Just a Moment!

Second Edition

BLESSINGS!
Aaron Zwiebel

Also by Ann Zwemer:

Professional Adjustments and Ethics for Nurses in India,
seven editions

Basic Psychology for Nurses in India

Just a Moment!

Longings

JUST A MOMENT!

Daily Reflections for Thinkers

Second Edition

Ann Zwemer

CROSSBOOKS
PUBLISHING

CrossBooks™
A Division of LifeWay
1663 Liberty Drive
Bloomington, IN 47403
www.crossbooks.com
Phone: 1-866-879-0502

First published by CrossBooks 09/10/2012

ISBN: 978-1-4627-2043-9 (sc)
ISBN: 978-1-4627-2045-3 (hc)
ISBN: 978-1-4627-2044-6 (e)

Library of Congress Control Number: 2012914220

Printed in the United States of America

This book is printed on acid-free paper.

To my three children
Frank, Mimi, and Kim,
who always make me proud.

FOREWORD

Ann Zwemer has enjoyed early morning walks for many years. As one who's been legally blind for over a decade (macular degeneration), walking is her primary mode of transportation but also a time for meditation. Often, she returned from her walk and began writing what I'd call distilled wisdom. She is able to convey in very few words enough insight to keep me mulling for a long time. That is a gift.

Ann often shared one or more of these reflections with me, and I was delighted when she published a year's worth. I gave copies to all my friends and enjoyed reading and thinking about these tidbits—one a day or several at a time. People who pick up the book in a doctor's waiting room call Ann and ask to buy their own copy or copies to share with others.

The insights in these reflections come from eight decades of living—growing up in a large family, becoming a nurse, training and writing textbooks for nurses in India as a missionary nurse, raising a family, and lots of church involvement (from church organist to church board president). The real foundation is her deep faith in God, which shows in the mix of pragmatism and spirituality found in these writings.

The fruit of her life and faith is these 366 updated reflections about life, love, happiness, sorrow, fear, joy, contentment, and faith. Ann has used them in a discussion group in her community and at the Braille Institute, where she both attends and teaches classes. They call us into a kind of dialogue with the author and with ourselves about a broad range of subjects. Read, think, and enjoy, and allow these reflections to add depth to your days.

—Reverend Diana Augspurger

PREFACE TO SECOND EDITION

"Just a Moment!" Daily Reflections for Thinkers, first published in 2005 (Vantage), is a collection of my personal reflections and favorite Scripture passages which gave meaning to my life for more than eighty-three years. Each reflection is written in one short sentence, which can be read in a moment, but is meant to be thought-provoking and meaningful. The reflections include thoughts about such subjects as age, anger, contentment, failure, God, happiness, justice, loss, love, peace, self-esteem, and time.

In this second edition of *Just a Moment!*, I have revised some of the original reflections, replaced others, and added a very useful subject index.

This calendar book is not marked by a specific year, so it can be used as a perpetual calendar. Many readers of the first edition tell me that they read the book every day, year after year. Some read the entire book in one sitting and then go back to the daily readings.

Each reflection has been written with great care to express what I believe is most important in life. Because I am legally blind, I have used large print, only two reflections on a page, to make reading easier for those who are visually impaired. I believe even those who are very pressed for time can take just a moment to reflect on something good and meaningful each day.

I am grateful to my reflections class at the Braille Institute, where the students actively discussed my reflections, sometimes disagreeing but always sharing.

I deeply appreciate all of the invaluable assistance from my good friend, Llona (La Nay) Kitzing, who so patiently went through this material again and again, contributing her own thoughts as we discussed each reflection, always helping me to "stay the course" to successfully complete this second edition.

I hope these thoughts will be meaningful to you, my readers, as you reflect upon your own lives.

Ann Zwemer

PREFACE TO FIRST EDITION

To write is a joy. To share is a joy. Hence, this little book. As small as it is, it represents seventy-five years of living and three years of writing. The thoughts may be familiar, but the arrangement of words is rhythmic and succinct. It is my hope that even people who are very busy will take a moment to read a thought each day. And, because I am legally blind, I hope others who cannot see well will appreciate being able to read a meaningful thought in a few words.

I am grateful to my family, both children and siblings, who have encouraged me in this venture. I am extremely thankful for friends who have taken their time and effort to read and critique this material. I deeply appreciate the support given to me by the Women's Fellowship of Lake San Marcos. I am especially grateful to my pastor, Reverend Diana Augspurger, for her help and affirmation.

I enjoyed the time I spent with two groups of adults who were willing to experiment with these reflections as they participated in discussion classes. One class for the visually impaired meets weekly at the Braille Institute in La Jolla, California. The other class consists of members of the United Church of Lake San Marcos, California. Our experience was remarkable and uplifting as, together, we grappled with how to become happier, more content, closer to God, more fulfilled, more patient, less lonely, and more loving. This is what we search for during our journey through life.

Finally, I thank God for walking so closely with me through the valley of grief and guiding me day by day from the threat of a life of emptiness to one of fullness and joy.

January 1

I want to make
today
the beginning
of something
special.

January 2

One resolution
I can keep
is to say
a prayer
before I sleep.

January 3

The only time
I have is
now.
Let today
be all
it can be.

January 4

It is a rare
valley of
failure
that has
no sign
of hope.

January 5

What I think
of myself
controls
what I become.
I *become*
as long as
I live.

January 6

My priorities
are reflected in
what I do,
because
I almost always
do what is
most important
to me.

January 7

Change
terrifies me,
even though
it chases
cobwebs and
boredom.

January 8

Be strong
and courageous.
Do not be afraid.
God will not leave you
or forsake you.

January 9

God
wants
my heart,
not
my stuff.

January 10

I can find
a substitute
for everything
except time.
Time is not
replaceable.

January 11

Fear and faith
are incompatible:
fear
paralyzes;
faith
empowers.

January 12

Though I cherish
an independent
lifestyle,
I must learn
to be content in
any lifestyle.

January 13

If I could see
the future,
my crises
of today
might seem
unimportant.

January 14

My whole
being
is affected
by the quality
of my
heartbeat.

January 15

Wisdom
is never
complete;
totally new
situations
continue
to arise.

January 16

A closed door
is just
as useful
for direction
as an
open door.

January 17

I reach
the mountaintop
only
by going
through
the valley.

January 18

I cannot
choose
how I feel;
I *can*
choose
how I behave.

January 19

Living
is
adjusting;
adjusting
is
living.

January 20

It is
up to me
to decide
who or what
will control
my life.

January 21

When faith
and feeling
part ways,
I need to follow
faith.

January 22

I have
only one life,
but many
choices
of how
to live it.

January 23

A new season
marks
the passage of time,
as a new year
marks
the passage of life.

January 24

Planning for
the letdown
after a big event
is part of
planning
the event.

January 25

I would be
more content
if most of
what I do
is that which
I do best.

January 26

Believing
Christ walks
with me
makes all things
tolerable
and all things
possible.

January 27

Though many may
pray for me,
only I
can establish
my relationship
with God.

January 28

There is
a big difference
between
a fence
and
a wall.

January 29

I should
daydream
only when
I am in
a safe
place.

January 30

I searched
for happiness
everywhere
before I found it
within
myself.

January 31

My worry
about
tomorrow
can ruin
my today.

February 1

Bitterness
and anger
have long roots
that can choke out
the rest of life.

February 2

There is a vast
difference
between
an acquaintance
and
a friend.

February 3

Any friend
who loves me
just as
I am
is a priceless
treasure.

February 4

There are
three things
that remain—
faith, hope, and love—
and the greatest
of these
is love.

1 Corinthians 13:13 LB

February 5

As an adult,
how I wish
I could sleep
like
a baby.

February 6

It is possible
to find
a measure of
contentment
in any
situation.

February 7

The bitterness
of sorrow
can be
sweetened
with time
and faith.

February 8

Love
always hurts…
at some
point.

February 9

Is
God
always
available
on demand?

February 10

It is hard
to be alone
when
something
extraordinary
happens.

February 11

I want
to love.
I need
to love.
Let love
not escape me!

February 12

I am born
into
a world of
separation.

February 13

Hurry
is the speed
at which
I often trip
and fall.

February 14

Love
does not
hold grudges
and will hardly
even notice
when others
do it wrong.

1 Corinthians 13:5 LB

February 15

For I am
convinced …
nothing
can separate me
from the
love of God.

Romans 8:38–9 LB

February 16

Patience
gained
is
frustration
lost.

February 17

I often
benefit
from
talking
to myself.

February 18

Even
in sadness,
I can find
an element
of gladness.

February 19

My love
for another
will give
that person
freedom
to be
that person.

February 20

Certain
outer activities
can quiet
my inner
spirit.

February 21

Self-fulfillment
happens
when I follow
God's plan
for my life.

February 22

How I spend
my time
and money
reflects
my priorities.

February 23

Money
can buy
most anything;
money
can ruin
most anything.

February 24

I need
to learn
to enjoy
being
alone.

February 25

If I behave
in a
loving way,
I can
become
a loving person.

February 26

I rarely
claim
the desires
of
my heart.

February 27

Though uninvited,
birthdays
always
show up
and
will hopefully
come again.

February 28

Time
is a mystery—
a tiny piece
of
eternity.

February 29

I often speak
to God;
I wish
I could hear
God
speak to me.

March 1

When trouble
strikes
I stop,
knowing
the world
must go on.

March 2

I talk so much
yet say so little,
leaving unsaid
that which is
most important.

March 3

Using
foul speech
shows
I have yet
to master
the language.

March 4

Amazing grace!
How sweet the sound!
… I once was lost
but now am found,
was blind,
but now I see.

John Newton

March 5

To be moved
by the Spirit
is
to be moved
to higher ground.

March 6

My judgment
of others
will likely change
when I find
myself
in their place.

March 7

Peace will
escape me
unless
I put
God in charge.

March 8

I judge
the behavior
of others
knowing
I can only
control my own.

March 9

It is easier
to feed
my body
than
to feed
my soul.

March 10

Feeling good
about myself
only lasts
if the feeling
comes from within.

March 11

When acutely ill,
I am not able
to pray
for myself
nor am I
lonely.

March 12

Positive
anticipation
is my most
powerful
motivator.

March 13

I am more
content
when
my positive
expectations
come true.

March 14

A secret
shared
is
no longer
a secret.

March 15

I hardly notice
the weight of
my cross,
because
others carry it
with me.

March 16

I never know
what's
around the corner
in space
or in time.

March 17

When I run
into trouble,
it helps
to remember
things could
be worse.

March 18

There
is no
retirement
for a
homemaker.

March 19

The pill I take
to rest
my body
rarely
rests
my soul.

March 20

The most
valuable things
are those
for which
I have
to wait.

March 21

When I am young,
I long to be
older.
When I am old,
I long to be
younger.

March 22

I will accept
change
if I know
certain things
will never
change.

March 23

Peace
comes to me
when
I am able
to rise above
petty
frustrations.

March 24

God is good
in every
life situation,
because
God is
always good.

March 25

Solitude
is often
where I find
the power of
the Spirit.

March 26

Spoken words
soon
fade away;
written words
go on
and on.

March 27

If my only
identity
is in my work,
I will be
miserable
in retirement.

March 28

Contentment
begins with
satisfaction
in my
personal
space.

March 29

Prayer can be
pleading,
praising,
thanking,
conversing—
even a lifestyle.

March 30

Using a cane
hurts
my pride.
Wouldn't a fall
hurt more?

March 31

When I find
God
in prayer,
I am on
holy ground.

April 1

How much
I want possessions
grows
with age
and diminishes
with age.

April 2

What
I want to do
is always
more attractive
than what
I have to do.

April 3

When I
am anxious
I remember,
*Because the Lord
is my shepherd,
I have everything
I need.*

April 4

Being alone
without
loneliness
can be
calming and
refreshing.

April 5

An inner peace
will hold me
steady
as I journey
through a world
of turbulence.

April 6

If I mean
"Thy will be done,"
I need to
give up
ownership of
that situation.

April 7

My body language
speaks
my inner
thoughts and
feelings.

April 8

To suffer
well
is
a great
achievement.

April 9

Acting out
forgiveness
makes it
easier
to forgive.

April 10

When my ego
hurts,
I want
to hurt
somebody else.

April 11

Sometimes
it is easier
to relate to the
sick and dying
than to
healthy people.

April 12

My life
is cradled
in providence
rather than
luck.

April 13

I no longer
fight aging
when I accept
my child as
my parent.

April 14

To forgive
is
to be
free.

April 15

Many things
can fill my
home;
only people
can fill
my heart.

April 16

I feel the
power of
daylight most
when
it dispels
my fears of
the night.

April 17

The scars of
personal
rejection
disfigure
my self-image.

April 18

My abilities
are limitless
if the
Spirit of God
lives in me.

April 19

God
is my Creator,
my Provider,
my Judge,
and my Forgiver.
God is also
my best friend.

April 20

If everybody
would keep the
Ten Commandments,
we would
live in
utopia.

April 21

My faith
is so
irrepressible;
the more
I give away,
the more
I have.

April 22

There is nothing
more reassuring
than
believing
God is here.

April 23

When the day ends,
never to return,
I wish
I had thought of that
when it began.

April 24

The older
I am,
the faster
I forgive.

April 25

Wanting to be
at the top
is an innate
human
desire.

April 26

When I can eat
for pleasure
rather than
necessity,
I am affluent.

April 27

Effective
prayer
takes
regular
practice.

April 28

Even as I plan
for tomorrow,
I feel time
slipping
through
my fingers today.

April 29

When I can
truthfully say,
"It's a blessing
to be handicapped,"
I have
overcome.

April 30

I am finished
with grieving
only
when I can
remember
without pain.

May 1

Having a
routine
is like the
"bread of life"
to my
mental health.

May 2

I realize the
true value
of anything
only
when I have
lost it.

May 3

It is comforting
to know
death
does not end
my relationships
with loved ones.

May 4

A feeling
of sadness
often comes
to me
right after
a big achievement.

May 5

To find a
kindred spirit
is to find
a very
special gift.

May 6

A parent
needs to teach
a child
how to live
and
how to die.

May 7

I can never
completely
close
the generation
gap.

May 8

Geographical
distance from
friends and
relatives
provides privacy,
freedom ...
and loneliness.

May 9

God
offers me
no
retirement
plan.

May 10

What others
think of me
seems important;
what I think
of myself
is most important.

May 11

When life
gives me
more time
for my children,
life gives them
less time for me.

May 12

When I admit
I made a mistake,
I am taking
the first step
toward
ending a conflict.

May 13

The deepest
longing
of my soul
is
to be
made whole.

May 14

The person
managing a home
manages
the most important
business
in the world.

May 15

Today, tell your
loved ones
you love them:
tomorrow,
they may not
be here.

May 16

To the handicapped,
privacy
and personal space
become
luxuries.

May 17

Ultimate
selfishness
is wanting others
to be
exactly
like me!

May 18

Nostalgia
leaves me
partly sad,
partly glad,
and only partly
satisfied.

May 19

When
in doubt,
do
nothing.

May 20

Human
freedom
is
always
limited.

May 21

Being ready
to die
is the first
step
in being ready
to live.

May 22

The better
I know myself,
the more
content
I can be.

May 23

Silence
is a world
of which
I know little;
I seldom
allow it to exist.

May 24

I have happiness
for a moment;
when it lasts longer,
I have joy;
when it
lasts the longest,
I have contentment.

May 25

The words I speak
are only a
fraction
of those
I leave
unspoken.

May 26

Before I say
what I think,
I should
think
again.

May 27

Give me
a task
and
I will
live!

May 28

As my
eye sight
becomes less
my
soul sight
becomes more.

May 29

The most
breakable
article of life
is the
personal
relationship.

May 30

Death is a
journey,
a process,
a release.
It is an end
and a beginning.

May 31

Discipline means
doing what I
should do
whether
I like it
or not.

June 1

Familiar strains
of music
soothe
my soul, especially
in times of
stress.

June 2

I am
most content
when I act
more than
I react.

June 3

All the surgery
in the world
cannot produce
a face-lift
equal to a
smile!

June 4

For every
negative
situation,
there is a
positive
life experience.

June 5

Physical pain,
never welcome,
gives
exquisite
relief
when it goes.

June 6

The world
of nature
is always
disrupted
by
my presence.

June 7

I cannot buy
inner beauty:
it
just
happens.

June 8

The "Me"
generation
has taught me
to be kinder
to myself.

June 9

Gut feelings
act as a
compass
guiding me
in the right
direction.

June 10

Marriage
makes
two people one:
sometimes
one spouse,
half a person.

June 11

A good laugh
reflects
good health,
especially
if I am laughing
at myself.

June 12

What I say
to others
does not speak
as clearly
as what
I do.

June 13

Setting goals
for
tomorrow
gives me
purpose
for today.

June 14

Most of what
I worry about
never
happens.

June 15

I usually
want to control
that to which
I give my
time or money.

June 16

The depth of
aloneness
felt by loving
widows or
widowers
is
unfathomable.

June 17

Pay all your debts
except
the debt of
love for others …
never finish
paying that!

Romans 13:8 LB

June 18

Competition
would not
exist
in a
perfect
world.

June 19

Stretching
my abilities
is like
warming up for
the rest of
life's journey.

June 20

My search
for perfection
is
always
hopeless.

June 21

To do something
well and say,
"It is good,"
reflects
a healthy
self-image.

June 22

The pain
of separation
is the price
I pay for
the joy of
togetherness.

June 23

I have a
lifelong conflict
between
keeping myself
for me or giving
myself away.

June 24

In the pursuit
of happiness,
I surprisingly find
more
is
less.

June 25

Making
errors
keeps
me
humble.

June 26

The deepest
longing
of my heart
is
to be
loved.

June 27

I could learn
new things
if I were
more willing
to risk
failure.

June 28

In the depth
of aloneness,
my deepest
longing
is
to be touched.

June 29

How I do
the things
I have to do
is so
important.

June 30

I live
most fully
when I give,
expecting
nothing
in return.

July 1

What bumps
in the road
do to me
depends upon
what I do
with them.

July 2

Wisdom is
knowing
what to do
and
what not to do.

July 3

I am restless
on the
outside
until I find peace
on the
inside.

July 4

Being just
means
I will share
my abundance
with others.

July 5

Being just
means
paying others
a fair price
for what
they do
for me.

July 6

Being just
means
asking only
fair interest
on my
investments.

July 7

Being just
means
making
interest-free
loans
to the needy.

July 8

Being just
means
I will not
waste resources
so that others
will have
enough.

July 9

Being just
means
I will not sue
those
who make
reasonable errors.

July 10

Being just
means
faithfully
paying taxes
and bills
on time.

July 11

Being just
means
loving
others
as I love
myself.

July 12

I rarely
do anything
without
mixed
motives.

July 13

Retirement
is scary
if working
has built
walls in
relationships
at home.

July 14

I say I want
equality
yet create
inequality
in much
of what I do.

July 15

I long for
freedom;
when I get it,
I tie myself
down.

July 16

I can forgive
others
more quickly
when I change
my focus
from me
to them.

July 17

I wish the
passage of time
could heal
a broken relationship
like it heals
a grieving heart.

July 18

Once
upon a time,
the medical patient
was
king!

July 19

I seem
to need God
most
when things
go wrong.

July 20

Everything
must
be
put
somewhere.

July 21

Blessings
may go
unrecognized
at first,
appearing
as burdens.

July 22

Few words
can
bring about
more peace
than
"I'm sorry."

July 23

Knowing
when to yield and
when to conflict,
is essential to
living in
peace.

July 24

Try to live
in peace
even if you must
run after it
to catch
and hold it!

1 Peter 3:11 LB

July 25

I need to be
set free
from the
bonds
of a poor
self-image.

July 26

When I join
a community,
their problems
become
my problems.

July 27

One choice
made
today
can influence
many
tomorrows.

July 28

The smaller
a group,
the easier
it is
to make
a decision.

July 29

In spite of
life's
uncertainties,
I plan
as though
it were certain.

July 30

I am most
miserable
when
my thoughts
focus wholly
upon me.

July 31

"Haves"
and "have-nots"
exist together;
always
apart.

August 1

My search
for inner
quietness
always ends
with searching
for God.

August 2

I'm so glad
I can reach
God
without
technology!

August 3

Of all the
things I wear,
my facial
expression
is most
important.

August 4

Fearlessness
of the young,
wisdom
of the old;
two facts of life
wondrous
to behold!

August 5

I need
many things;
I want many more;
I struggle
to know the
difference.

August 6

Although pride
produces
self-respect,
it also can
produce
arrogance.

August 7

I recognize
feelings
in others
more easily
than in
myself.

August 8

Gambling
thrives
on our desire
to become
rich
quickly.

August 9

Old habits
give me
comfort and
security,
begging me
not to change.

August 10

I can
find
opportunity
in almost
any
obstacle.

August 11

Competition,
the great
motivator,
always produces
losers.

August 12

A circle
is formed
only when
both ends
are joined and
sealed.

August 13

I can never
predict
exactly
what I will
think, do, or say
next.

August 14

I deal
courageously
with big things,
then
trip up on
little things.

August 15

I look
on the
outside
how I feel
on the
inside.

August 16

I often see life
and other people
as strange, while I
see myself
as normal.

August 17

Feelings
come to me
unbidden;
I bid them
to stay
or go.

August 18

Language
is the great
unifier
and the great
divider!

August 19

Loneliness
waits to
embrace me
unless
I reach out
to others.

August 20

Overuse
of anything
will cause
a cramp
in something.

August 21

Good conversation
needs
a balance of
speaking and
listening.

August 22

I'm always
in conflict
with
somebody
in some way.

August 23

Where
I am going
is more important
than
from where
I have come.

August 24

I can change
bad habits
more easily
if I replace
them with
good habits.

August 25

Crossing
cultural barriers
has become
a necessity,
though it was once
a novelty.

August 26

What I ask
from God
and what
I receive
may be
different.

August 27

Men have tamed,
or have trained,
every kind of animal—
but no human being
can tame
the tongue.

James 3:7 LB

August 28

Thinking
holds me
steady
as the winds
of feeling
blow.

August 29

It is good
to wear out
my walking shoes
before
they get dirty.

August 30

Buying anything
for a
good price
still
gives me
great pleasure.

August 31

Technology
would be
an amazing
gift
if I only knew
how to use it.

September 1

Even a beautiful
sunset
makes me sad
when I realize
the day is over,
gone forever.

September 2

I never ask
for
as much as
God
can provide.

September 3

Worry is like
a tiny trickle
of water
undermining
a huge rock.

September 4

How happy
our homes
would be if
we treated our families
as well as
we treated our guests.

September 5

Making money
should not
replace
service
to humanity.

September 6

I am blind
when
I do not see;
I am blind
when
I do not
understand.

September 7

If I am too busy
to rest
one day a week,
I should
re-evaluate
what I am doing.

September 8

I seek security
by joining
groups,
though these groups
may deny
security to others.

September 9

Envy and jealousy
are friends:
they do not
live comfortably
in a
secure person.

September 10

The older
I get,
the harder
it is
to say
good-bye.

September 11

Forgiving
means
forgetting:
wiping
the slate
clean.

September 12

Making an error
is okay:
it means
I'm still
active.

September 13

Working well
together
makes
any task
easier.

September 14

Dislike
can be changed
to like
through
open
communication.

September 15

To be needed
is important;
to be wanted
as well
is ideal.

September 16

Though
I understand
much of life,
so much
remains
a mystery!

September 17

The loneliness
of leadership
is inevitable:
nobody
can please
everybody.

September 18

My chores
seem easier
if I do the
toughest one
first.

September 19

I cannot
talk
and
listen
at the
same time.

September 20

Poverty is
as undesirable
to God
as it is
to man.

September 21

Humility
is not often
found
in the
prosperous.

September 22

The richest
country
in the world
still produces
poverty and
homelessness.

September 23

Anything
is possible
if you
have faith.

Mark 9:23 LB

September 24

When I make
a mistake,
the right
answer
stays with me
for life.

September 25

Learning
means
changing:
how I think,
what I do.

September 26

While I learn
much
from reading,
I remember
most
from doing.

September 27

I can understand
a situation
more clearly
when
I distance myself
from it.

September 28

It's a rare
situation
in which
I cannot feel
thankful
for something.

September 29

I am free
to put
whatever
I please
into my mind.

September 30

When I open
my heart
to a person,
I am opening
my heart
to God.

October 1

From birth
I travel
with loss,
knowing
I will never
lose the
love of God.

October 2

I should always
get rid of anger,
even if it
motivates me
to do good.

October 3

Human resilience
is best shown
by one's capacity
to rise above
the worst
circumstances.

October 4

Loneliness
in my heart
longs for people;
loneliness
in my soul
longs for God.

October 5

Keeping
too busy
is one way
of running away
from life.

October 6

Unless I use
my personal
talents,
I will
lose them.

October 7

I can be
more accepting
of others
if I understand
why they do
what they do.

October 8

When I find
myself
overloaded,
I must remember
I almost always
have a choice.

October 9

Times
have changed,
but
human nature
has not.

October 10

When grief
tears me apart,
I long to be
cradled
in the loving
arms of God.

October 11

I choose
conflict
over silence
if the issue
is important
enough.

October 12

Because
it feels good
to help others,
I should
allow others
to help me.

October 13

Wisdom is
more important
when I am
feeling up
than when I am
feeling down.

October 14

What I do
with
what I have
reflects
my responsibility
to others.

October 15

All I have
comes from
God:
all I have
belongs to
God.

October 16

I give easily
to charity
from
my abundance
because
I give
leftovers.

October 17

When I put
someone
on a pedestal,
I expect
that person
to be perfect.

October 18

Knowing
how to enter
the personal space
of those
who
are hurting
is an art.

October 19

Money is a
necessity.
Money is a
gift.
Money is
power.

October 20

I need
to control
what comes into
my mind.
My thoughts
make me
what I am.

October 21

I see myself
aging
on the outside,
even though
I feel no older
on the inside.

October 22

My
personal space
is to other space
as my kitchen
is to
my living room.

October 23

When my thinking
is rigid
and I feel
very comfortable,
I'm getting
old!

October 24

Doing something
meaningful
is like a
salve
to the pain
of loneliness.

October 25

Young adults
expound
so freely.
They honestly
believe
they know
everything.

October 26

I need
faith,
because
there are
so many
unknowns.

October 27

I give to
God
when
I give to
people.

October 28

I pray for
peace;
I pray for
harmony;
I pray …
and pray …
and pray.

October 29

My journey
through life
as a Christian
is that of
a pilgrim
in a foreign land.

October 30

What
I think
determines
much of
what
I feel.

October 31

I can get rid of
anger
more quickly
if I am willing
to admit
I am angry.

November 1

I can never help
all needy people,
but
I can help
a few.

November 2

I think God
would agree
when I say,
"Life is not fair,"
but God would add,
"I will be there."

November 3

I go on living
by still giving,
even when
my world
consists of only
me in my abode.

November 4

An attitude
of gratitude
will fill
my life
with joy and
satisfaction.

November 5

Tears
are
safety valves
for the weak
and the strong.

November 6

The more
I give
to others,
in any form,
the more
I receive.

November 7

The emptiness
of loss
can be filled
by recognizing
the value of
what is left.

November 8

Maturity
gives me the
capacity
to smile
through
tears.

November 9

I should
always
be ready
to meet
God
face-to-face.

November 10

I eagerly
seek a
long life,
even as I
reject the
aging process.

November 11

Ask,
and you will be given
what you ask for.
For everyone
who asks,
receives.

Matthew 7:7–8 LB

November 12

I cannot choose
who I am
when I am born,
but I can choose
who I am
when I die.

November 13

Carelessness
will
always
waste
my time.

November 14

The beauty
of something seen
at a distance
may be lost
when it is seen
up close.

November 15

I can smile
on the inside
without
laughing
on the
outside.

November 16

My contentment
depends more
upon
what I do
than
what others do.

November 17

My shrinking world
is one of my
greatest
challenges
as I grow
older.

November 18

Slowing down
with age
is so comfortable that
I question
the busyness
of my
younger years.

November 19

Having
company
is a great
motivator!

November 20

Compassion,
unlike pity,
gives
a helping
hand.

November 21

I will always
give thanks
in good times
and
in bad.

November 22

If I am asked,
"Am I my
brother's
keeper?"
The answer
is
"Yes!"

November 23

When
my friend
died,
I lost
a piece of
my inner
being.

November 24

Dark thoughts
will get
darker
if I do not
let them go.

November 25

A complete
family tree
will have
at least
one
bad apple.

November 26

It is easy
to put
myself
on a pedestal
when I give
to charity.

November 27

The price tag
on something
will not always
reflect
its
value.

November 28

Appreciating
little things
gives me
a big
measure
of happiness.

November 29

It is easier
to accept
a Supreme Being
than it is
to accept Christ,
a personal God.

November 30

God gives us
greater gifts
than
we request,
but we must
claim them.

December 1

Learning
new things
will ease
the pain
of losing things
I once enjoyed.

December 2

How quickly
I gather possessions;
how slowly
I give them up;
yet, I leave
this world
with none.

December 3

Life is
a poignant
mixture of
sadness
and
gladness.

December 4

A gift
is a gift
only
when it is
received
and accepted.

December 5

The greatness
of God
is far beyond
my imagination.

December 6

I have at least
one
personal gift
that I must
identify and
use.

December 7

When I affirm
a positive trait
in another person,
I give
a gift of
great value.

December 8

When I think
of my entire life,
it is a gift
to know
I am now
where I should be.

December 9

As long as
I have a purpose
for living,
I will find
some measure
of happiness.

December 10

True success
is measured
by what
I have done
with what
I have been given.

December 11

Although my god
could be
anything,
I want
my god
to be God.

December 12

I see hope
as a flicker
of light
when I feel
surrounded
by darkness.

December 13

If I expect more
of myself
than what
I'm able to do,
I will not
be content.

December 14

I am tempted
to keep
the best
of anything
for myself.

December 15

I need
to learn
when
to put away
my ego.

December 16

I find myself
when
I give
myself
away.

December 17

When I try to lead
a good life,
I am surprised
to find
God
shows no
favoritism.

December 18

It is a gift
to have
some emptiness,
because
only emptiness
can be filled.

December 19

Happiness is …
a goal,
a gift,
an obsession.
It is never
completely
a possession.

December 20

Christmas brings
the giving
of gifts,
the best of which
is
myself.

December 21

When the sadness
of Christmastime
inevitably visits me,
I let it
come.
Then I let it go.

December 22

The gift wrap
on my love
for others
should have
no strings
attached.

December 23

It is almost
impossible
for me to grasp
the richness of
my intangible
possessions.

December 24

The greatest
gift
of all time
is
God with us.

December 25

God's gift is here
for you.
Take it:
find life in all
its fullness.

December 26

How I wish
I could
grasp time
to keep it
from
slipping away!

December 27

I throw away
gift wrap
but cherish
the love
behind each gift.

December 28

Living longer
is a gift
only if it
includes
living
better.

December 29

The Lord
turn His face
toward you
and give you
peace.

Numbers 6:26 NIV

December 30

The end of the year
seems to come
too slowly
for the young and
too quickly
for the old.

December 31

Every day
of the year
is a gift;
all of time
is sacred.

Just a Moment!

Second Edition
INDEX

Ego: Apr. 10

Failure(s): Jan. 4; Jun. 27; Dec. 15
Faith: Jan. 11, 21; Feb. 7; Apr. 21; Oct. 26
Fear: Jan. 11
Feel(ings): Jan. 18, 21; Apr. 7, 16; Jun. 9;
    Aug. 7, 15, 17, 28; Oct. 30
Forgive(ness): Apr. 9, 24; Jul. 16; Sept. 11
Free: Sept. 29
Freedom: Jul. 15
Friend(ship): Feb. 2, 3; Apr. 19; Nov. 23
Frustration: Mar. 23
Future: Jan. 13

Generation (gap): May 7; Jun. 8
Gift: Dec. 6, 7, 8, 18, 19, 20, 24, 25, 27, 28, 31
Giving: Nov. 3, 6; Dec. 20
Goals: Jun. 1
God: Jan. 9, 27; Feb. 21, 29; Mar. 7, 24, 31;
    Apr. 17, 18, 19, 22; Jul. 19; Aug. 1, 2, 26;
    Sept. 2, 20, 30; Oct. 1, 4, 15, 27; Nov. 2, 9, 30;
    Dec. 11, 17, 24, 25
Grace: Mar. 4
Gratitude: Nov. 4
Grief: Apr. 30; Oct. 10
Grieving: Jul. 17

Habit(s): Aug. 9, 24
Happi(ness): Jan. 30; May 24; Jun. 24; Sept. 4;
    Nov. 28; Dec. 9, 19

Heart: Feb. 26; Apr. 15; Jun. 26; Sept. 30
Home: May 14
Hope: Mar. 5; Dec. 12
Humility: Sept. 21
Hurry: Feb. 13

Joy: May 20, 24; Jun. 22
Just(ice): Jul. 4–11

Language: Aug. 18
Laugh: Jun. 11
Leadership: Sept. 17
Learning: Sept. 25
Listen: Sept. 19
Loneliness: Mar. 11; Apr. 4; May 8; Aug. 19;
    Sept. 17; Oct. 4, 24
Losing: Dec. 1
Loss: Oct. 1; Nov. 7
Love: Feb. 4, 8, 11, 14, 19, 25; May 15;
    Jun. 17, 26; Dec. 22, 27

Mental health: May 1
Money: Feb. 22, 23; Oct. 19
Mother: May 4
Motivator(s): Mar. 12; Aug. 11; Nov. 19
Myself: Feb. 1; Jun. 11, 15, 23; Jul. 11; Oct. 7,
    21; Nov. 26; Dec. 13, 14, 16, 20

New Year: Jan. 1, 2, 23
Nostalgia: May 18

Old(er): Mar. 21; Oct. 23; Nov. 17; Dec. 30
Opportunity: Aug. 10

Parent: May 6
Patience: Feb. 16
Peace: Mar. 7, 23; Apr. 5, 17; Jul. 3, 22, 23, 24;
    Oct. 28; Dec. 29
Perfection: Jun. 20
Personal gift: Dec. 6
Personal space: May 16, Oct. 22
Plan: July 29
Possessions: Dec. 2
Pray(er): Jan. 27; Mar. 29, 31; Apr. 27; Oct. 28
Priorities: Jan. 6; Feb. 22
Pride: Mar. 30; Aug. 6
Providence: Apr. 12

Receive(s): Nov. 11

Sacred: Dec. 31
Sad(ness): Feb. 18; Mar. 5; May 18; Sept. 1;
    Dec. 3, 21
Secure: Sept. 9
Security: Aug. 9; Sept. 8
Self: Jun. 7, 21; Aug. 6
Self-esteem: Jan. 5; Mar. 10, 27; Apr. 17;
    May 10, 27; Jul. 25
Self-fulfillment: Feb. 21
Separation: Feb. 12
Silence: May 23

Sleep: Feb. 5
Sorrow: Feb. 7
Soul: Mar. 9, 19; May 13, 28; Jun. 1, Oct. 4
Speech: Mar. 3; May 25
Spirit: Feb. 20; Mar. 25; May 5
Success: Dec. 10

Tears: Apr. 14; Nov. 5
Thank(ful): Sept. 28; Nov. 21
Time(s): Jan. 3, 23; Feb. 2, 7, 22, 28; Jul. 17;
    Oct. 9; Nov. 13; Dec. 26
Trouble: Mar. 1, 17

Wisdom: Jan. 15; Jul. 2; Oct. 13
Work(ing): Sept. 13
Worry: Jan. 31; Jun. 14; Sept. 3

Young(er): Mar. 21; Oct. 25; Dec. 30

CPSIA information can be obtained at www.ICGtesting.com
Printed in the USA
BVOW011250071012

302328BV00002B/2/P